Never
Leave the
House
Naked

And 50 other
Ridiculous Fashion Rules

COLOPHON

BIS Publishers
Het Sieraad
Postjesweg 1
1057 DT Amsterdam
The Netherlands
T (+) 31 (0)20-515 02 30
F (+) 31 (0)20-515 02 39
bis@bispublishers.nl
www.bispublishers.nl

ISBN 978-90-6369-214-8

Ridiculous Design Rules is a concept developed
by Lemon Scented Tea and commissioned by
Premsela, Dutch Platform for Design and Fashion
(www.premsela.org).

Editorial Director: Anneloes van Gaalen
(www.paperdollwriting.com)
Designed by: Lilian van Dongen Torman
(www.born84.nl)

BISPUBLISHERS

Never Leave the House Naked

And 50 other Ridiculous Fashion Rules

CONTENTS

INTRODUCTION

The international fashion police is a force to be reckoned with. Armed with a seemingly endless list of rules, it dictates all the do's and don'ts and acts as both judge and jury in dealing with those guilty of committing a crime against fashion. But while some of the rules that are enforced by the fashion-conscious are nothing short of ridiculous, others serve more as words of wisdom that can prevent people from committing a fashion faux-pas.

This book contains fifty-one rules – like 'Dress Your Age', 'When in Doubt Wear Red', 'Shoes and Bags Must Always Match' and 'Never Wear Tights with Open-toed Shoes' – which can be twisted, broken or ignored altogether. Our aim is not to list all the rules that you need to adhere to. Nor do we take sides in the whole rules debate. After all, creativity knows no bounds and therefore it seems rather ridiculous to restrict that creativity by sticking to a couple of age-old rules.

However, in some cases the rules seem more like the basic principles of dress that should be loved, honored and obeyed. Rest assured that whichever side of the fence you sit on in this whole fashion rules debate, you're bound to find this book a source of inspiration, comfort or joy.

Also available in the *Ridiculous Design Rules* series are *Never Use White Type on a Black Background and 50 other Ridiculous Design Rules* and *The Medium is the Message and 50 other Ridiculous Advertising Rules*.

For future publications on ridiculous design rules, we are looking for submissions. If you know about web design or typography rules, email them to us at: info@ridiculousdesignrules.com. And while you're at it, check out our website www.ridiculousdesignrules.com.

Do not mix two seasons in one outfit

rule
01

The idea is that your bottom half should match the upper part of your body, which in theory actually makes a lot of sense. 'Cause why on earth would you want to mix a micro-mini with a turtleneck or wear a pair of legwarmers with your skimpy summer dress?

"When Michelle Obama wore a sleeveless dress for the '60 Minutes' interview with her husband after the election, a number of people asked me about going sleeveless in winter. They seemed quite puzzled, in fact. Lots of women go sleeveless year-round, but when dresses came back into fashion a few years ago, the look became more popular. I think it's a personal choice. Mrs. Obama has well-toned arms, and she frequently throws on a cardigan. I happen to be a fan of sleeveless for evening occasions, but, again, if you harbor doubts about the shape of yours, don't bother."
Cathy Horyn (1957), American fashion critic

"Somebody next to me whispers…that the world is divided into two categories: women who wear boots in summer and women who don't. Good to know."
Stefano Tonchi (1959), Italian-born style editor

Fashion always comes back around

What goes around comes around and nowhere is that as (painfully) obvious as in the field of fashion where every couple of years ideas are regurgitated and presented as new.

"The novelties of one generation are only the resuscitated fashions of the generation before last."
George Bernard Shaw (1856-1950), Irish playwright

"Fashion is about today. You can take an idea from the past, but if you do it the way it was, no one wants it."
Karl Lagerfeld (1938), German fashion designer

"I think David Bowie said, 'Shoulder pads are the bell-bottoms of the '80s.' And just as bell-bottoms reared their head again in fashion, so will shoulder pads."
Marc Jacobs (1963), American fashion designer

"Fashion is more usually a gentle progression of revisited ideas."
Bruce Oldfield (1950), British fashion designer

rule
03

Shoes are the foundation of all fashion

It's all about the shoes. Or, as Marilyn Monroe put it: "Give a girl the right shoes and she can conquer the world."

———

"To be carried by shoes, winged by them, to wear dreams on one's feet is to begin to give reality to one's dreams."
Roger Vivier (1907-1998), French shoe designer

"I don't know who invented the high heel, but all men owe him a lot."
Marilyn Monroe (1926-1962), American actress and singer

"My shoes are special shoes for discerning feet."
Manolo Blahnik (1942), Spanish-born British fashion and shoe designer

"Boots send a different message than shoes do. They have a real Amazonian appeal. They're the tough shoe."
Valerie Steele (1955), American fashion historian

"High heels oblige women to have a certain body language and attitude. I don't like a laissez-faire attitude. A consciousness of the body is good; that's why I like high heels – you're less frumpy with them on."
Christian Louboutin (1963), French shoe designer

Don't over accessorize

The implication of this rule is that, when it comes to accessories, less is more. In order to avoid accessory overload, better take Coco Chanel's (1883-1971) advice to heart and "take one thing off before you leave the house."

———

"Know, first, who you are, and then adorn yourself accordingly."
Epictetus (AD. 55-AD. 135), Greek philosopher

"No elegance is possible without perfume. It is the unseen, unforgettable, ultimate accessory of fashion that heralds your arrival and prolongs your departure."
Coco Chanel (1883-1971), French fashion designer

"Accessories are important and becoming more and more important every day. They can completely change the look of an outfit, and women like the idea of having a wardrobe that's versatile."
Giorgio Armani (1934), Italian fashion designer

"I enjoy hats. And when one has filthy hair, that is a good accessory."
Julia Roberts (1967), American actress

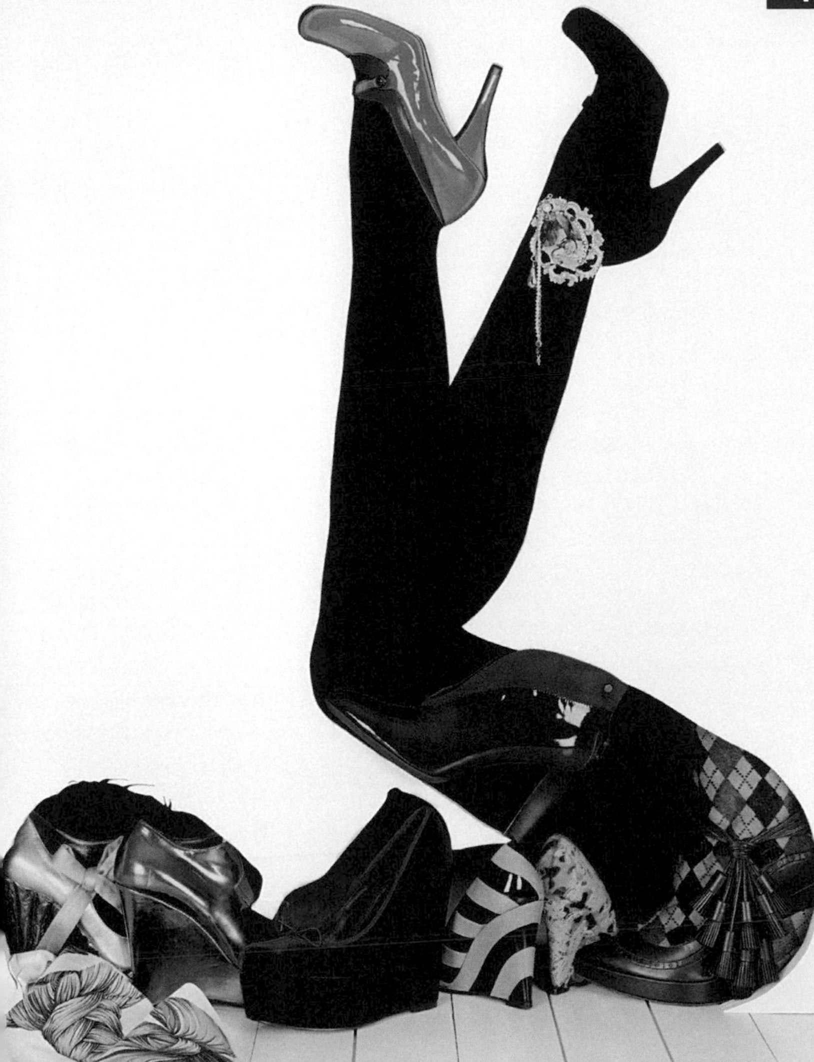

Underwear isn't outerwear

It started with Brando and Dean, who lit up the silver screen in their white tees, and it culminated in females everywhere exposing their thong for all the world to see. Thankfully, butt cleavage is no longer in fashion but underwear has been widely accepted as outerwear since the 1980s when Madonna donned layers of lace, when homeboys started exposing their briefs by wearing their pants down low, and when Gaultier and Westwood featured the old corset in their catwalk shows.

"I came out here with one suit and everybody said I looked like a bum. Twenty years later Marlon Brando came out with only a sweatshirt and the town drooled over him. That shows how much Hollywood has progressed."
Humphrey Bogart (1899-1957), American actor

"I've always thought of the T-shirt as the Alpha and Omega of the fashion alphabet."
Giorgio Armani (1934), Italian fashion designer

"I think there's something incredibly sexy about a woman wearing her boyfriend's T-shirt and underwear."
Calvin Klein (1942), American fashion designer

"In the eighties, designers such as Jean Paul Gaultier and Vivienne Westwood knew how to bring the corset back into fashion. The corset became an outergarment; a visible and, especially in the beginning, sensational element in their creations."
Herman Roodenbrug (1951), Dutch cultural historian

"Invest as much time, effort and money into buying underwear as you do in your visible wardrobe; never let your underwear become an afterthought."
Gok Wan (1974), British fashion consultant

"Fashions fade, style is eternal."

French fashion designer Yves Saint Laurent (1936-2008) not only brought the world wonderful designs, he also came up with this one-liner that over time has become something of a fashion mantra.

"Oh, never mind the fashion. When one has a style of one's own, it is always twenty times better."
Margaret Oliphant (1828-1897), Scottish writer

"Sometimes the eye gets so accustomed that if you don't have a change, you're bored. It's the same with fashion, you know. And that, I suppose, is what style is about."
Bill Blass (1922-2002), American fashion designer

"'Style' is an expression of individualism mixed with charisma. Fashion is something that comes after style."
John Fairchild (1927), American publisher of Women's Wear Daily and W

"The difference between style and fashion is quality."
Giorgio Armani (1934), Italian fashion designer

"The goal I seek is to have people refine their style through my clothing without having them become victims of fashion."
Giorgio Armani (1934), Italian fashion designer

"I've always been about style for people, not 'you're going to wear this outfit,'... It was the way you put yourself together and the imagination, not buying this number off the rack, but the way you wear it."
Ralph Lauren (1939), American fashion designer

"Style to me is about an attitude to dressing and a certain confidence in knowing what really suits you."
Matthew Williamson (1971), British fashion designer

Your coat should always be longer than your skirt

This is one of those old etiquette rules that might have made perfect sense in the early 50s of the last century but now might seem a tad dated.

———

"So long as you buy a knee-length [coat], rather than a short, mid-thigh version (ugly with knee-length skirts), you can wear it with skirts as well as trousers. (Both are comic with long dresses, though.)"
Jess Cartner-Morley, British fashion editor

"The general rule is for the jacket to just cover your entire seat. Another yardstick relates coat length to arm length: the hem of the jacket should end near the tip of your thumb when your arms are relaxed in order to a- void a gorilla-esque effect."
Tom Julian, Nordstrom Guide to Men's Style *(2009)*

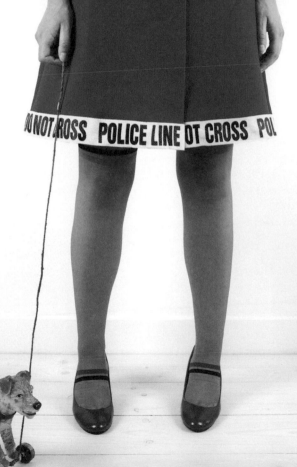

DRESS FOR COMFORT, NOT FOR FASHION

It's amazing the amount of discomfort dedicated followers of fashion are willing to put up with. From tight corset dresses to painful pumps: apparently suffering in style remains *en vogue*.

———————

"Luxury must be comfortable, otherwise it is not luxury."
Coco Chanel (1883-1971), French fashion designer

"I buy my shoes a size too small. I like the way it feels."
Karl Lagerfeld (1938), German fashion designer

" I base my fashion taste on what doesn't itch."
Gilda Radner (1946-1989), American actress and comedian

"Design is a constant challenge to balance comfort with luxury, the practical with the desirable."
Donna Karan (1948), American fashion designer

"When I get home I get undressed and take my heels off. I design homewear: I like to wear things that are comfy but pretty. I don't think just because one is at home one should be scruffy."
Loulou de la Falaise (1948), French fashion muse and designer

"A woman is never sexier than when she is comfortable in her clothes."
Vera Wang (1949), American fashion designer

"We've become obsessed with comfort. I actually don't like that. I think you should suffer sometimes to be attractive and beautiful."
Tom Ford (1961), American fashion designer

"Corsetry should always be comfortable. Held tightly in its grip, of course, it is a kind of bondage, but a very reassuring kind as it aligns the spine and balances the torso."
Mr. Pearl (1962), South African corsetier

"I don't think my shoes should be uncomfortable for the sake of fashion. If a woman is uncomfortable, it's reflected in her face and it doesn't leave a nice aperture. But I don't like shoes that look comfortable."
Christian Louboutin (1963), French shoe designer

Never wear tights with open-toed shoes (or socks in sandals)

rule
09

Is there anything quite as upsetting as seeing a woman wearing a peep-toe shoe with pantyhose? Or even worse, a grown man wearing sandals and socks?

"Mr. Obama is known to sport his BlackBerry in a holster on his belt, which to many is the sartorial equivalent of wearing socks with sandals."
Brad Stone (1971), American journalist

"Summer brings out those singularly unattractive 'American Tan' nylon 'foot-liners' that look like catering hair-nets for the feet. What's more, they inevitably tear, don't stop your feet smelling and poke out from all shoes unattractively despite their supposed invisibility."
Karen Homer, British fashion journalist and author of Things a Woman Should Know About Shoes *(2008)*

"Sandals, socks and shorts are no longer a fashion faux pas as long as you are a twenty-something male model or could pass for one."
Karen Homer, British fashion journalist and author of Things a Woman Should Know About Shoes *(2008)*

39

Logos suck!

Never wear a visible logo… unless you're paid to do so.

———

"Just because you have a logo plastered across your chest doesn't mean it's good."
Giorgio Armani (1934), Italian fashion designer

"It's fun seeing my label on someone's behind – I like that."
Calvin Klein (1942), American fashion designer

"I think it's completely impossible [to eliminate the logo] today. The recognition of the brand is too important. The more you want to enlarge your business, the more you have to use your logo."
Miuccia Prada (1949), Italian fashion designer

"A few years ago, I started taking the logos off my clothes just because they were so distinctive, and it had been a few years, and I figured that it was time. But then when I met with customers they said, 'Put them back!' They liked the logos. So I put them back on because of customer input."
Tommy Hilfiger (1951), American fashion designer

"Vuitton is a status symbol. It's not about hiding the logo. It's about being a bit of a show-off."
Marc Jacobs (1963), American fashion designer

"You know what killed fashion off? Those f...ing logos. They brought it down to the level of advertising, and that's not fashion, that's Letraset."
Alexander McQueen (1969), British fashion designer

Cleavage or legs, never both

Showing a bit of leg or breast is fine, but ladies who want to avoid over-exposure know they'd better not show both at the same time.

"Nothing goes out of fashion sooner than a long dress with a very low neck."
Coco Chanel (1883-1971), French fashion designer

"Your dresses should be tight enough to show you're a woman and loose enough to show you're a lady."
Edith Head (1897-1981), American costume designer

"I often think that a slightly exposed shoulder emerging from a long satin nightgown packed more sex than two naked bodies in bed"
Bette Davis (1908-1989), American actress

"We undress men and women, we don't dress them anymore."
Pierre Cardin (1922), Italian-born French fashion designer

"The greatest concubines in history knew that everything revealed with nothing concealed is a bore."
Geoffrey Beene (1924-2004), American fashion designer

"There is a real vulgarity in the way women dress at the moment. They show off too much and try too hard. They don't understand where the line is between sexy and vulgar. I know where that line is."
Roberto Cavalli (1940), Italian fashion designer

"The secret of toe cleavage, a very important part of the sexuality of the shoe. You must only show the first two cracks."
Manolo Blahnik (1942), Spanish-born British fashion and shoe designer

"We love sensual ironic fashion and that always includes cleavage."
Domenico Dolce (1958) and Stefano Gabbana (1962), Italian fashion designers

Never leave the house naked

rule
12

"The first thing the first couple did after committing the first sin was to get dressed. Thus Adam and Eve started the world of fashion, and styles have been changing ever since." There you have it, the naked truth, as published in *Time Magazine* back in 1963.

"The finest clothing made is a person's skin, but, of course, society demands something more than this."
Mark Twain (1835-1910), American author

"When I free my body from its clothes, from all their buttons, belts, and laces, it seems to me that my soul takes a deeper, freer breath."
August Strindberg (1849-1912), Swedish playwright and author

"All dress is fancy dress, is it not, except our natural skins?"
George Bernard Shaw (1856-1950), Irish playwright

"A woman who doesn't wear lipstick feels undressed in public. Unless she works on a farm."
Max Factor (1877-1938), Polish-born cosmetics entrepreneur

"A woman is closest to being naked when she is well dressed"
Coco Chanel (1883-1971), French fashion designer

"Clothes are inevitable. They are nothing less than the furniture of the mind made visible."
James Laver (1899-1975), British author and art historian

"Naked I came, and naked I leave the scene, And naked was my pastime in between"
J. V. Cunningham (1911-1985), American poet

"I tell people all the time I want to be buried naked. I know there will be a store where I'm going."
Nan Kempner (1930-2005), American socialite

Shoes and bags must always match

There was a time when a real lady wouldn't dare leave the house without donning a pair of shoes that perfectly matched her bag. Etiquette no longer requires such coordination. Lipstick and nail polish, carpet and drapes, shoes and bags: these days, none of them need to match.

———

"Shoes and bags can be made from the same material, but shouldn't be of the same design. Three straps on the shoe and three matching straps on the bag doesn't work."
Jan Jansen (1941), Dutch shoe designer

"[Designing shoes] is totally different from a bag because there are so many more elements, so many of the parts must be created separately. I adore shoes and bags and I love the idea of designing shoes along with the bags."
Hester van Eeghen (1958), Dutch bag and shoe designer

"I love looking hooked-up! Just like when I was a little kid, my shoes match my bag that matches my belt – only now it's likely to be matching Gucci or D&G."
Kimora Lee Simmons (1975), American model and creative director Phat Fashions

"Whereas fashion once dictated the rules – like matching handbags and shoes – it now breaks them to move forward."
Carmel Allen, author The Handbag: To Have and To Hold *(2002)*

You never get a second chance to make a first impression

First impressions matter. After all, the world's a stage and all of us mere players in what can best be described as a continual social performance, which features socially-acceptable masks and disguises in the form of decorum and fashionable dress.

"Fashion is the science of appearance, and it inspires one with the desire to seem rather than to be."
Henry Fielding (1707-1754), British novelist and playwright

"If people turn to look at you on the street, you are not well dressed."
George Bryan 'Beau' Brummel (1778-1840), British dandy

"The only way to atone for being occasionally a little over-dressed is by being always absolutely over-educated."
Oscar Wilde (1854-1900), Irish poet, playwright and author

"Women dress alike all over the world: they dress to be annoying to other women."
Elsa Schiaparelli (1890-1973), Italian-born French fashion designer

"You can have whatever you want if you dress for it."
Edith Head (1897-1981), American costume designer

"In a Balenciaga you were the only woman in the room – no other woman existed."

Diana Vreeland (1903-1989), American fashion editor

"You have a much better life if you wear impressive clothes."
Vivienne Westwood (1941), British fashion designer

"It's always the badly dressed people who are the most interesting."
Jean Paul Gaultier (1952), French fashion designer

"Dressing up. People just don't do it anymore. We have to change that."
John Galliano (1960), Gibraltarian-British fashion designer

"Sometimes I'm really dressed up, and it really turns me on."
Isaac Mizrahi (1961), American fashion designer

"I'd like to believe that the women who wear my clothes are not dressing for other people, that they're wearing what they like and what suits them. It's not a status thing."
Marc Jacobs (1963), American fashion designer

"DON'T FOLLOW TRENDS, START THEM."

Frank Capra (1897-1991), American film director best known for producing such cinematic classics as *Mr. Smith Goes to Washington* and *It's A Wonderful Life*, was once quoted as saying: "My advice to young filmmakers is this: Don't follow trends, Start them!"

"Don't be into trends. Don't make fashion own you, but you decide what you are, what you want to express by the way you dress and the way you live."
Gianni Versace (1946-1997), Italian fashion designer

"Trying too hard to follow every trend? You want to look fashionable and put-together, not like you hit every sale rack this season."
Tommy Hilfiger (1951), American fashion designer

"There are tons of people who are late to trends by nature and adopt a trend after it's no longer in fashion. They exist in mutual funds. They exist in clothes. They exist in cars. They exist in lifestyles."
Jim Cramer (1955), American television personality

"Follow sound business trends, not fashion trends."
Janice Dickinson (1955), American model and self-proclaimed first supermodel

"Trends for us are not as important as an inspiration. We do not set out to design something within a trend or to set a trend. We create something because it is at the forefront of our minds and it needs to be expressed."
Viktor Horsting (1969) and Rolf Snoeren (1969), Dutch fashion designers Viktor & Rolf

"I have always said I hate trends, but that is really hypocritical of me. It is my duty as a designer to create and set trends. Without trends, there is no competition, and no competition means no fun, no money and, ultimately, no survival."
Craig Robinson (1972), American fashion designer

"It's hard to go with a trend. As soon as it's out, everyone picks it up. It's important to stay true to yourself. Have fun with fashion instead of letting it dictate."
Estella Warren (1978), Canadian actress and model

Black is slimming

Fashion journalists, designers and the weight-challenged individual all have one thing in common: their love of black clothes.

"Scheherezade is easy; a little black dress is difficult."
Coco Chanel (1883-1971), French fashion designer

"I wear only black. Black is slimming and doesn't show stains. Jackie O. wore black. Audrey Hepburn wore black."
Ilene Beckerman (1935), American advertising executive-turned-writer

"There's no Chanel collection without black. (It) will never exist. Who can live without some black clothes."
Karl Lagerfeld (1938), German fashion designer

"Fashionistas adore black – hence the term 'fashion nuns'."

Cathy Horyn (1957), American fashion critic

"Most women feel that black is kind to them. When you're in a hurry to get dressed, black always works. It might take a little more time to find the right turquoise dress."
Candy Pratts Price (1949), American fashion director of Style.com

"[In the 1950s] black had a lot to do with 'being correct'. This was a period when fashion went mass in a big way. It wasn't just the socialites and the upper middle class wanting to be fashionable; it was the housewife."
Valerie Steele (1955), American fashion historian

"I had done all these really wild collections and colors and short skirts, and that disgusted me. I wanted to do something serious, and black is very, very serious."
Alice Roi (1976), American fashion designer

Dress your age
(not your shoe or waist size)

Age-old, slightly ageist adage that calls for age-appropriate dress.

———————

"Clothes that are too young paradoxically make their wearer look older. Remember that the interesting men of the world like women who appear youthful but who are not pathetic carbon copies of the girls they were. On the other hand, clothes that are too sophisticated do not imbue the youthful wearer with the femme fatale look she longs to achieve but tend, on the contrary, to give her a comically childlike appearance."
Edna Woolman Chase (1877-1957), American editor-in-chief Vogue

"The correlative of act your age has often been dress your age. Which is only to put in abeyance what, with everlasting fascination, fashion covers up: however you dress – man, woman, man-woman, or… what? – you are inevitably dressed with age."
Herbert Blau (1926), American author, theater director and professor

"Nothing is a question of age. If you have good health you can be fantastic and seductive until 90. It's a question of eyes, a good mind, a good soul."
Sonia Rykiel (1930), French fashion designer

"It's not about age. It's about taste, and it's about lifestyle. I believe women of all ages can wear anything."
Ralph Lauren (1939), American fashion designer

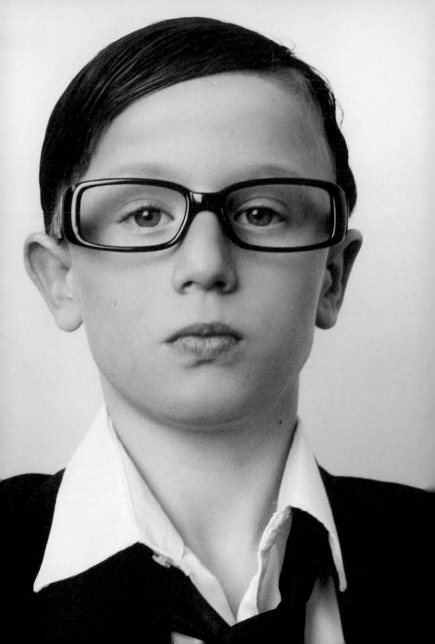

"I never think much of my age, I just get dressed and wear things that suit me at the moment."

Loulou de la Falaise (1948),
French fashion muse and designer

"I see lots of mothers buying high fashion and couture for toddlers – I think it's disgusting. There's Gucci and Burberry for three-year-olds. I just don't believe children should wear designer clothes at this age."
Iman Bowie (1955), Somali super-model

"Age shouldn't affect you. It's just like the size of your shoes – they don't determine how you live your life! You're either marvelous or you're boring, regardless of your age."
Steven Morrissey (1959), British singer and songwriter

... *is the new black*

The actual origins of the phrase remain something of a mystery, although Diana Vreeland (1903-1989) usually gets the credits. Back in 1962 the renowned fashion editor was shown an Eastern-looking piece of pink fabric after which she exclaimed: "Pink is the navy blue of India." Over time navy blue was replaced by a whole range of colors. It wasn't until the early 1980s that the color black was introduced into the catchphrase.

_____

"Actually, pale-pink salmon is the only color I cannot abide. Although, naturally, I adore PINK. I love the pale Persian pinks of the little carnations of Provence, and Schiaparelli's pink, the pink of the Incas. And, though it's so vieux jeu I can hardly bear to repeat it, pink is the navy blue of India".
Diana Vreeland (1903-1989), Ameri-can fashion editor

"It seems to me it was only last year that brown was supposed to be the new black. And the year before it was navy blue. Maybe next year, black will be the new black. I'm ready. I've been ready for 10 years."
Ilene Beckerman (1935), American advertising executive-turned-writer

"Naturally pink is the navy blue of India because it's the cheapest of all dyes."
Gianfranco Ferré (1944-2007), Italian designer

"I'm not that interested in fashion... When someone says that lime-green is the new black for this season, you just want to tell them to get a life."
Bruce Oldfield (1950), British fashion designer

...he new white is the new purple is the new orange is the new mage
the new red is the new auburn is the new orange is the new green is
w Atomic tangerine is the new apricot is the new bondi blue is the
nelian is the new denim is the new ecru is the new fallow i
denrod is the new heliotrope is the new indigo is the new jade is the
aki is the new lavender is the new maize is the new ochre is the
vine is the new pear is the new raw umber is the new russet is the
l brown is the new tangerine is the new vermillion is the new whea
new xanadu is the new wisteria is the new viridian is the new viol
new ultramarine is the new upsdell red is the new turquoise is the
lian pink is the new thistle is the new teal **is the new black** is
taupe is the new slate grey is the new silver is the new sienna is the
cking pink is the new sepia is the new scarlet is the new sapphire is
saffron is the new ruby is the new rose is the new robin egg blue is
razzmatazz is the new pumpkin is the new platinum is the new pers
n is the new persian red is the new periwinkle is the new peach is
payne's grey is the new orchid is the new olive is the new myrtle is
mint green is the new mauve is the new maroon is the new malachi
new mahogany is the new lime green is the new lemon is the new l
ue new kelly green is the new jade is the new ivory is the new gamb
ue new fuchsia pink is the new flax is the new emerald is the new ecr
new desert sand is the new cyan is the new crimson is the new cordo
e new cerulean is the new celadon is the new carnelian is the new cos
is the new byzantium is the new burgundy is the new buff is the
s is the new bistre is the new aquamarine is the new alizarin is the
is the new navy is the new acid yellow is the new grey is the new bro
e new white is the new purple is the new orange is the new magent
new red is the new auburn is the new orange is the new green is the
nic tangerine is the new apricot is the new bondi blue is the new ca
is the new denim is the new ecru is the new fallow is the new golden
e new heliotrope is the new indigo is the new jade is the new khaki is
lavender is the new maize is the new ochre is the new olivine is the
is the new raw umber is the new russet is the new seal brown is the
erine is the new vermillion is the new wheat is the new xanadu is the
wisteria is the new viridian is the new violet is the new ultramarin
ew upsdell red is the new turquoise is the new thulian pink is the
le is the new teal is the new taupe is the new slate grey is the new silve
ew sienna is the new shocking pink is the new sepia is the new scarle
ew sapphire is the new saffron is the new ruby is the new rose is the
egg blue is the new razzmatazz is the new pumpkin is the new pl
is the new persimmon is the new persian red is the new periwinkle is
peach is the new payne's grey is the new orchid is the new olive is

Less is more

The motto is often credited to architect Ludwig Mies van der Rohe (1886-1969), but was actually mentioned first in the 1855 poem *Andrea del Sarto* by Robert Browning (1812-1889). In fashion 'less is more' alludes to the Minimalist look – that is, simple, clean-lined couture – as well as the ever-shrinking models that wear it.

"It's what you leave off a dress that makes it smart."
Nettie Rosenstein (1890-1980), American fashion designer

"I despise simplicity. It is the negation of all that is beautiful."
Norman Hartnell (1901-1979), British fashion designer

"All it takes are a few simple outfits. And there's one secret: The Simpler The Better."
Cary Grant (1904-1986), British-born American actor

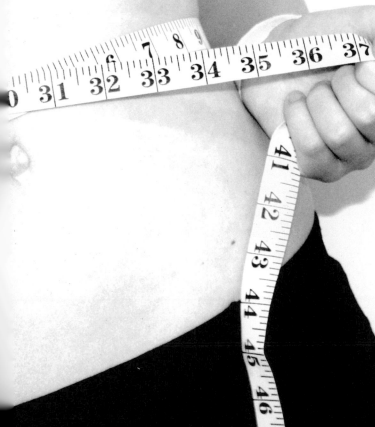

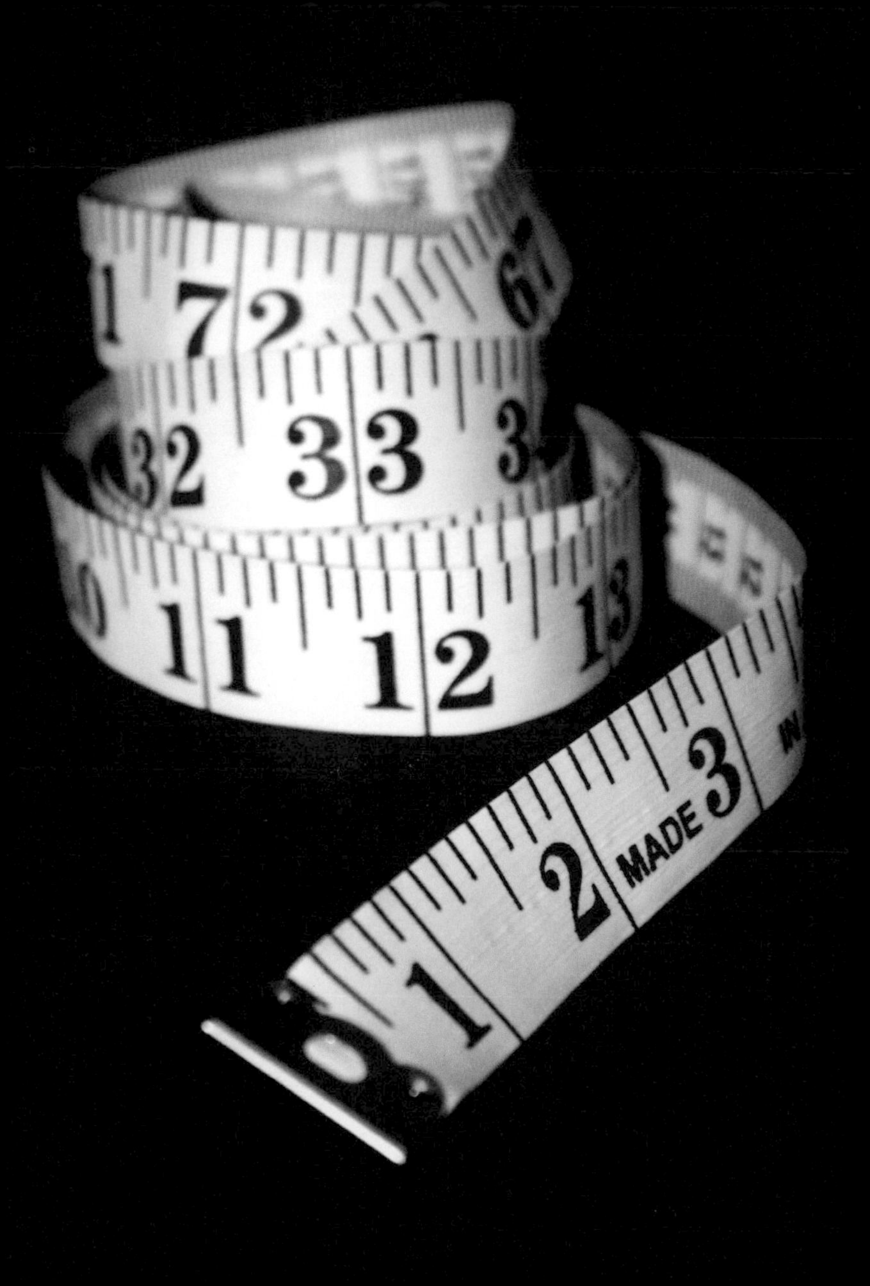
MADE

"Buy less, think more."

Jil Sander (1943), German fashion designer

"I think some people would love to be able to make the clothes I make – and of course, I do influence them, but they keep simplifying, and minimalism doesn't quite work."
Vivienne Westwood (1941), British fashion designer

"Minimalism without a sense of quality and class doesn't mean very much."
Jil Sander (1943), German fashion designer

"As the president of the Council of Fashion Designers of America, I represent the designers. And while we can by no means take the blame for eating disorders, we can play our part in addressing this important issue."
Diane von Fürstenberg (1946), Belgian-born fashion designer

"The leading cause of death among fashion models is falling through street grates."
Dave Barry (1947), American author

"Most of the Vogue girls are so thin, tremendously thin, because Miss Anna (Wintour) don't like fat people."
André Leon Talley (1949), American editor-at-large at Vogue

If the shoe fits, buy it in every color

rule 20

British design critic Stephen Bayley (1951) once said that "in an age robbed of religious symbols, going to the shops replaces going to the church." Shopping as a religious experience. It's certainly one way of describing a money-oriented consumer society that thrives on at least four of the seven deadly sins: lust, envy, gluttony and greed.

"Some women won't buy anything unless they can pay a lot."
Helena Rubinstein (1870-1965), Polish cosmetics entrepreneur

"Women usually love what they buy, yet hate two-thirds of what is in their closets."
Mignon McLaughlin (1913-1983), American journalist and author

"I did not have three thousand pairs of shoes. I had one thousand and sixty."
Imelda Marcos (1929), former First Lady of the Philippines

"Fashion flourishes on surplus, when someone buys more than he or she needs."
Stephen Bayley (1951), British design critic

"I think people should hang on to the things they like. They don't need closets full of clothes."
Laura Ashley (1925-1985), British designer

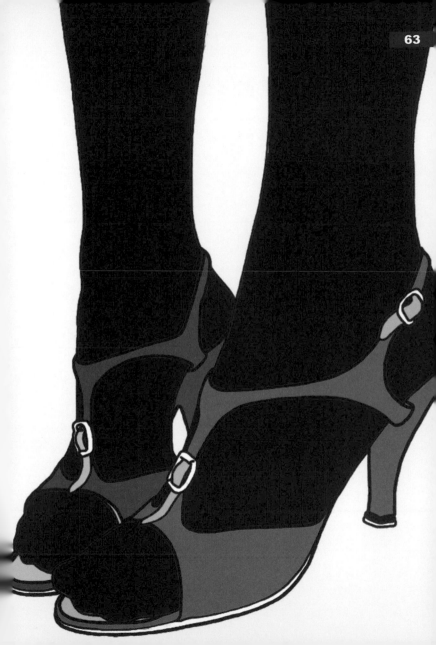

Elegance is the privilege of age

In her 1964 book *A Guide to Elegance* French style guru and former director of the Nina Ricci fashion house, Genevieve Antoine Dariaux wrote words of encouragement for ageing women everywhere: "There is a saying in France, 'Elegance is the privilege of age' – and thank heavens it is perfectly true. A woman can be elegant until the end of her days."

"Elegance is not the prerogative of those who have just escaped from adolescence, but of those who have already taken possession of their future."
Coco Chanel (1883-1971), French fashion designer

"Elegance is innate. It has nothing to do with being well dressed. Elegance is refusal."
Diana Vreeland (1903-1989), American fashion editor

"A woman who is utterly stupid will always find it extremely difficult to become truly elegant."
Madame Genevieve Antoine Dariaux (1914), French style guru

"We must never confuse elegance with snobbery."
Yves Saint Laurent (1936-2008), French fashion designer

"Isn't elegance forgetting what one is wearing?"
Yves Saint Laurent (1936-2008), French fashion designer

"For me, elegance is not to pass unnoticed but to get to the very soul of what one is."
Christian Lacroix (1951), French fashion designer

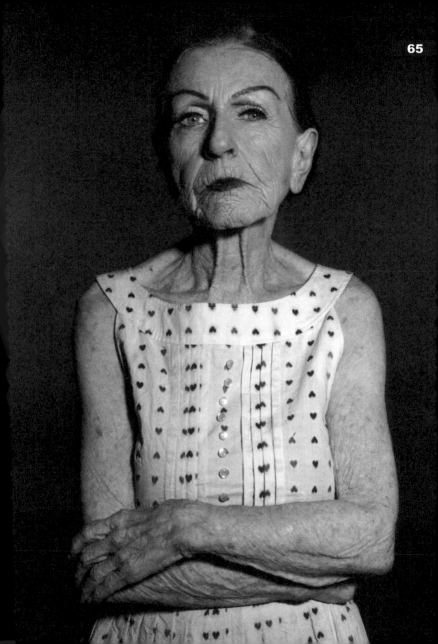

Clothes make the man

KEITH

BRIAN

Widely-used and known saying that we have Roman rhetorician Marcus Fabius Quintilianus (c. A.D. 35-95), a.k.a. Quintilian, to thank for.

"Those who make their dress a principal part of themselves, will, in general, become of no more value than their dress."
William Hazlitt (1778-1830), British writer

"Clothes and manners do not make the man; but when he is made, they greatly improve his appearance."
Henry Ward Beecher (1813-1887), American clergyman and social reformer

"Clothes make the man. Naked people have little or no influence on society."
Mark Twain (1835-1910), American author

"What a strange power there is in clothing."
Isaac Bashevis Singer (1902-1991), Polish-born American author

"A man should look as if he had bought his clothes with intelligence, put them on with care, and then forgotten all about them."
Hardy Aimes (1909-2003), British fashion designer and dressmaker to Queen Elizabeth II

"Even the most conservative man in the world at the office may dress with a bit more originality in bed. Besides, he should consider the fact that, just as he hates to see his wife in a long flannel nightgown, she may not feel like sleeping next to a convict in stripes."
Madame Genevieve Antoine Dariaux (1914), French style guru

"While clothes may not make the woman, they certainly have a strong effect on her self-confidence – which, I believe, does make the woman."
Mary Kay Ashe (1918-2001), American entrepreneur and founder of Mary Kay Cosmetics

DON'T WEAR WHITE AFTER LABOR DAY

You shouldn't wear linen in winter. You shouldn't wear suede shoes in summer. And you shouldn't wear white after Labor Day.

———————

"[Stepping out in white shoes between Labor Day and Easter would be a faux pas,] except, of course, if you lived in Florida or a tropical climate and it was hot. If it was cold in Florida, then no."
Letitia Baldrige (1925), American etiquette expert

"Once, on a plane, I was deeply of-
fended by a passenger seated near me
who was guilty of the ultimate fashion
violation – wearing summer white after
Labor Day and before Memorial Day…
Did he deserve to die for his hideous
outfit? Would the readers of *Women's
Wear Daily* and *GQ* have rallied wildly
to my defense if I had blown him
away?"
*John Waters, (1946), American film-
maker*

"Those traditional rules about not wearing white after Labor Day absolutely
do not apply to white jeans — they are
a staple."
Bruce Pask, American fashion editor

"The rule is, after Memorial Day and
before Labor Day, you are allowed
to wear white shoes… A lot of people
think it is white clothes. That is not
true."
*Diann Catlin, American etiquette
consultant*

"My stringent right-wing fashion belief
that white still can NEVER be worn
before Memorial Day or after Labor
Day turned into a motive for murder
in *Serial Mom*."
*John Waters, (1946), American film
maker*

[Juror # 8 is talking on a payphone,
when Beverly comes up behind her
and grabs the phone from her]
Beverly Sutphin: You can't wear
white after Labor Day!
Juror # 8: That's not true anymore.
Beverly Sutphin: Yes it is! Didn't
your mother tell you? Now you know.
[She whacks her in the face with the
phone]
Juror # 8: No! Please! Fashion has
changed!
Beverly Sutphin: No... it hasn't.
[She hits her again]
Scene from Serial Mom

Never wear white to a wedding

The white wedding dress was popularized in the Western world by Queen Victoria after she married her beloved Albert in one back in 1840. Since then wedding guests have been told not to detract from the blushing bride by showing up in white.

"Talk six times with the same single lady and you may get the wedding dress ready."
Lord Byron (1788-1824), British Poet

"There is something about a wedding-gown prettier than in any other gown in the world."
Douglas William Jerrold (1803-1857), British playwright and journalist

"My grandfather Frank Lloyd Wright wore a red sash on his wedding night. That is glamour!"
Anne Baxter (1923-1985), American actress

"To have the bridesmaids flouncing down the aisle in black dresses is a travesty of taste. A bride is a bride the first time around. The white dress and the white veil are symbolic. So many people are breaking the rules that people don't know what the rules are."
Letitia Baldrige (1925), American etiquette expert

"Never outshine the bride unless she's marrying your ex-lover."
Trinny Woodall (1964) & Susannah Constantine (1962), British fashion advisors and television presenters

"At my cousin's wedding last summer I spent more on my outfit than the bride did. I wore Luke Hall jeans, shoes from b Store, a Miu Miu printed shirt with a mismatched belt and tie, and a cream backless waistcoat. It looked like someone had thrown up on me. An old woman asked my dad if he thought I had got dressed in the dark. The whole thing cost just over a grand."
Henry Holland (1983), British fashion designer

Redheads shouldn't wear red

The rule is that redheads shouldn't wear red. Or pink. Or salmon. Or orange. Or purple. Or any other color or shade that could potentially clash with their ginger locks.

"It's supposed to be taboo. [But] if redheads aren't supposed to wear red clothes, then that's exactly what I do."
Patty Mitropoulos, American fashion editor

"Once in his life, every man
is entitled to fall madly in love
with a gorgeous redhead."

Lucy Ball (1911-1989), American comedian and actress

"It's a misconception that redheads
shouldn't wear red lipstick. Bright,
flame-red hair is best suited to bluer
reds, while those with a deeper, more
auburn coloring can experiment with
warm-based tones."
Poppy King (1972), Australian cosmetics entrepreneur

WHEN IN DOUBT WEAR RED

Nothing like a bit of bright red to liven up your wardrobe. The color red evokes strong emotions and also has a wide range of connotations, which might very well explain why American fashion designer Bill Blass (1922-2002) once said: "When in doubt wear red."

"Red is the ultimate cure for sadness."
Bill Blass (1922-2002), American fashion designer

"Women usually prefer to wear black at events, because it makes them feel safe. However, if there's one woman wearing red, she will inevitably be the eye-catcher of the evening. It's as though the room is suddenly illuminated, simply perfect for a grand entrance."
Valentino (1932), Italian fashion designer

"When in doubt, make it big. If still in doubt, make it red."
Michael Bierut (1957), American graphic designer and critic

"Red is one of the strongest colors, it's blood, it has a power with the eye. That's why traffic lights are red I guess, and stop signs as well... In fact I use red in all of my paintings."
Keith Haring (1958-1990), American artist

"An assistant in the office always used to wear the same color red lipstick and matching nail polish. One day I asked to borrow it and coated the bottom of a pair of stilettos just to see what it would look like, et voilà! I loved the dramatic red color against the clean line of the shoe. It was the most beautiful red I'd ever seen. Now it's my hallmark."
Christian Louboutin (1963), French shoe designer

NO DENIM WITH DENIM

I like my blue jeans as much as the next person, but wearing denim head to toe is best left to rodeo cowboys, country singers and soccer moms. No offense.

———

"Blue jeans are the most beautiful things since the gondola."
Diana Vreeland (1903-1989), American fashion editor

"The jean! The jean is the destructor! It is a dictator! It is destroying creativity. The jean must be stopped!"
Pierre Cardin (1922), Italian-born French fashion designer

"I have often said that I wish I had invented blue jeans: the most spectacular, the most practical, the most relaxed and nonchalant. They have expression, modesty, sex appeal, simplicity – all I hope for in my clothes."
Yves Saint Laurent (1936-2008), French fashion designer

"Jeans represent democracy in fashion."
Giorgio Armani (1934), Italian fashion designer

"A designer is only as good as the star who wears her clothes."

There's no denying we live in a celeb-obsessed culture. Celebrities are the new Royals, serving as both entertainers and style icons for the masses. Endorsement deals are made in the hope that the celebrity will breathe new life into a dying brand or put the spotlight on an up-and-coming designer. The red carpet is the pinnacle of celebrity endorsement with famous faces dressed head to toe in designer wear, which they are contractually bound to rave about to the eagerly-awaiting press. Wonder what American costume designer Edith Head (1897-1981), who coined the above-mentioned rule, would have made of all this?

"I don't get the whole fascination with copying celebrities either. Surely it's more fun to find something that suits your own personality."
Celia Birtwell (1941), British textile designer

"Fashion is now completely celebrity-obsessed and moves at an incredibly fast pace."
Ashish Gupta (1973), Indian designer

"Although we don't necessarily agree with it, celebrity endorsement has also certainly become an important PR tool for established fashion houses, as well as young designers."
Bruno Basso (1978) and Christopher Brooke (1974), Brazilian-British design duo Basso & Brooke

DEBBIE HARRY

rule
29

IMITATION IS THE HIGHEST FORM OF FLATTERY

It's a fine line between inspiration and imitation. And almost nowhere is that line as blurred as in the world of fashion, thanks to high-street copies of catwalk designs and the multi-billion dollar counterfeiting industry.

"Fashion is something barbarous, for it produces innovation without reason and imitation without benefit."
George Santayana (1863-1952), Spanish-American philosopher and poet

"Being copied is the ransom of success."
Coco Chanel (1883-1971), French fashion designer

"Actually I am very glad that people can buy Armani — even if it's a fake. I like the fact that I'm so popular around the world."
Giorgio Armani (1934), Italian fashion designer

"I am a great believer in copying; there has never been an age in which people have so little respect for the past."
Vivienne Westwood (1941), British fashion designer

"By passing [an anti-counterfeiting] law, we emphasize the value of designs."
Diane von Furstenberg (1946), Belgian-born fashion designer

"A COPY CAN BE INTERESTING, BAD, CHEAP OR GOOD, BUT IT IS STILL A COPY."

*Laudomia Pucci (1961),
daughter of Italian designer Emilio
'Prince of Prints' Pucci*

"Copies, they are another way of being accessible. Of course, it upsets you initially, but it's a sign that what you are doing makes sense to people. That's important to me, because fashion should help people, not add extra problems."
Miuccia Prada (1949), Italian fashion designer

"When a design is copied, it is flattery, but when a designer's approach is copied, then it is scary."
Hussein Chalayan (1970), Turkish Cypriot fashion designer

"It's a very fine line of what is a copy and what is inspiration."
Zac Posen (1980), American fashion designer

FUR IS WORN BY BEAUTIFUL ANIMALS AND UGLY PEOPLE

Emotions tend to run high at the mere mention of the word fur. There is a huge divide in the fashion world between those who deem the use of animal skin immoral and those who insist on using and wearing animal skin.

In their war on fur, animal rights group PETA (People For The Ethical Treatment Of Animals) has called in the help of animal-loving celebrities like Pamela Anderson and Eva Mendes, who vouched they'd rather go naked than wear fur, which in some cases really isn't much of a stretch. PETA also came up with the above-mentioned slogan, which could very well end up becoming part of the unofficial rules book.

"Cruelty is one fashion statement we can all do without."
Rue McClanahan (1934), American actress

"The animals of the world exist for their own reasons. They were not made for humans any more than black people were made for white, or women created for men."
Alice Walker (1944), American author

"I HATE VOGUE EDITOR ANNA WINTOUR BECAUSE SHE BULLIES YOUNG DESIGNERS AND MODELS TO USE AND WEAR FUR."

Pamela Anderson (1967), Canadian actress

"I think Vogue's support of fur absolutely helped the fur industry. And at the time when fur sales were really suffering, we put [supermodel] Linda Evangelista on the cover in a blue fur. I think fur is an important part of our business. I love fur. I love the fancy of it. I love what designers are doing with it in terms of accessories and colors. We totally supported it and will continue to support it."
Anna Wintour (1949), British-American editor-in-chief Vogue

"Well I don't do leather and I don't do fur and it's not just because I don't eat animals or that I think that half a billion animals a year shouldn't be killed for the sake of fashion. It's because I also believe very much in the connection between fur and leather and the environment. There's a huge connection. Now, I think more and more people will start to take notice of that – the use of water for tanneries, the chemicals that are used – there's a huge impact environmentally."
Stella McCartney (1971), British fashion designer

"People who don't like fur can p**s off. I love fur. It's a beautiful, natural product from animals."
Julien MacDonald (1971), British fashion designer

FASHION IS ART

Whether or not you agree that fashion is art, there's no denying that there is an art to dressing well. And while it's a form of art that few truly master, it has the potential to create nothing short of masterpieces.

"It doesn't matter one damn bit whether fashion is art or not. You don't question whether an incredible chef is an artist or not – his cakes are delicious and that's all that matters."
Sonia Rykiel (1930), French fashion designer

"I think fashion is an art form – you might call it decorative or applied art as opposed to fine art, but what's the distinction? Because the same amount of artistic expression goes into clothes, a piece of pottery or a painting."
Zandra Rhodes (1940), British fashion designer

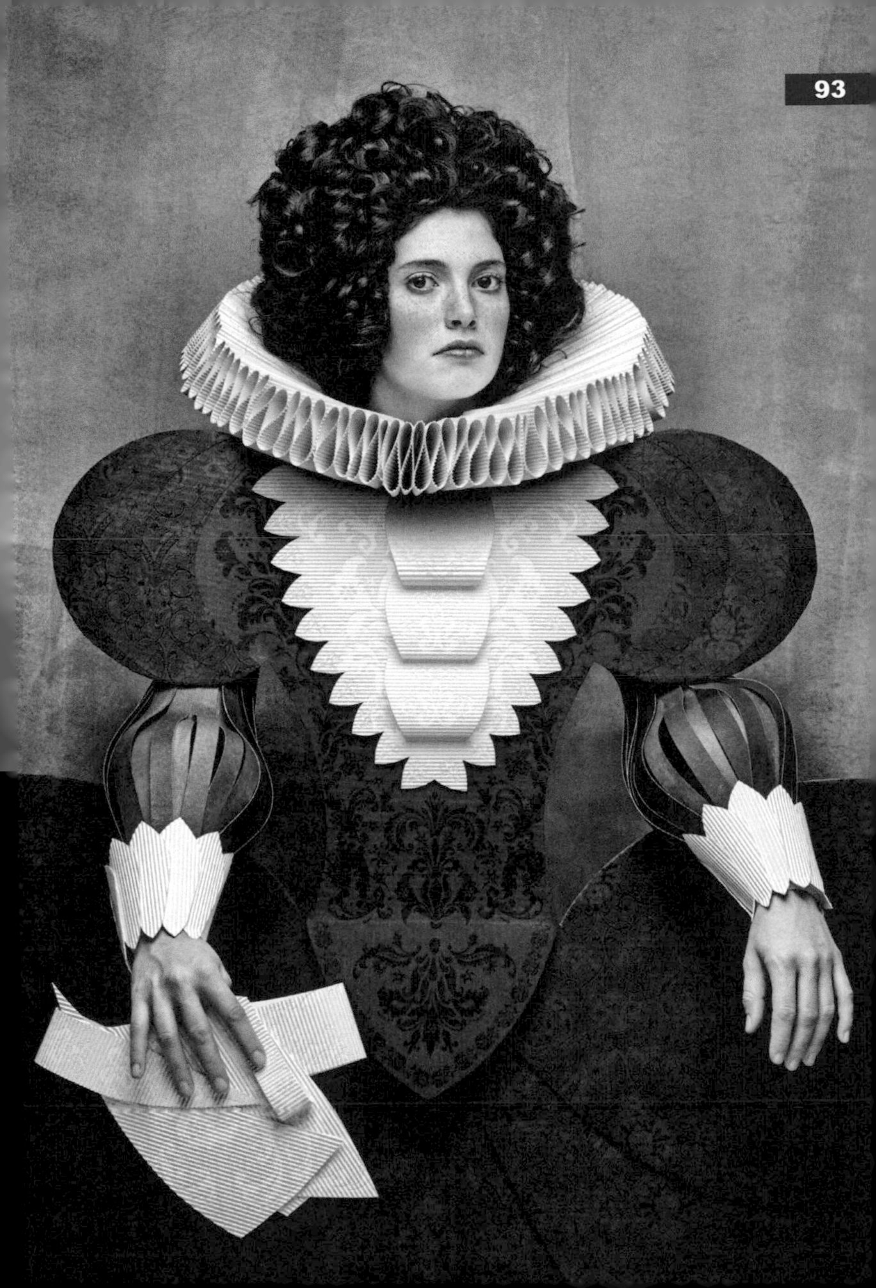

"ART AND FASHION ARE ONE AND THE SAME TO ME, INTRINSICALLY LINKED."

Wolfgang Joop (1944), German fashion designer

"A designer can be very creative, but art is something that stands by itself, and fashion is something you sell."
Miuccia Prada (1949), Italian fashion designer

"Fashion has a practical purpose, whereas art does not. The result may be as gorgeous as a vintage Balenciaga ball gown or an eloquent political metaphor for its time, but it is still an item of clothing intended to be worn."
Alice Rawsthorn (1958), British design critic

"As a fashion designer, I was always aware that I was not an artist, because I was creating something that was made to be sold, marketed, used, and ultimately discarded. True artists – and I do think there are some fashion-designer artists – create because they can't do anything but create. There is no purpose to their work other than expression."
Tom Ford (1961), American fashion designer

"The acceptance of the art world, that was not something we actively pursued. A lot of that… happened. We felt contented with that for a long time. It's important for us to have more platforms to express ourselves. We still do a lot of exhibitions. We still curate. But fashion is always the centre."
Viktor Horsting (1969), Dutch fashion designer and one half of Viktor & Rolf

Never Wear Checkers on TV

The camera not only adds 10 pounds, it also distorts your carefully-coordinated look. If you wear certain patterns on TV – like checkers – they can end up 'dancing' on screen. We won't bore you with the technical details behind this phenomenon. Just stick to wearing solids and you'll be fine.

"Until I was 50 I ignored my body, but then I did a television show and saw myself bloated in a tuxedo. Since then, I have worked out with a trainer for an hour-and-a-half every morning."
Giorgio Armani (1934), Italian fashion designer

"Sometimes cameras and television are good to people and sometimes they aren't. I don't know if it's the way you say it, or how you look."
Dan Quayle (1947), former American Vice President

"Back in the day, newspeople sat behind desks. Now they do full-body shots... I try to update every season with something fresh, like these shoes. They heighten and lengthen me, so you might see them on television if I'm daring. Because the camera really does add 10 pounds."
Alina Cho (1971), American CNN correspondent

THE CLIENT IS KING

The customer might not always be right but he (or she) is king (or queen). The client plays a vital role in the fashion game of supply and demand. After all, clothes, shoes and other fashion accessories are all meant to be worn, felt and indeed bought by customers.

————

"We don't want to push our ideas on to customers, we simply want to make what they want."
Laura Ashley (1925-1985), British designer

"Now is the most exciting time in fashion. Women are controlling their destiny now, the consumer is more knowledgeable, and I have to be better every single day."
Oscar de la Renta (1932), American fashion designer

"Fashion, as we knew it, is over; people wear now exactly what they feel like wearing."
Mary Quant (1934), British fashion designer

"I design for real people. I think of our customers all the time. There is no virtue whatsoever in creating clothing or accessories that are not practical."
Giorgio Armani (1934), Italian fashion designer

"I'm a little naive but I don't like the idea of showing things that you don't sell in a store. It's not being honest to the client. For me, fashion is something that people can enjoy and wear."
Dries van Noten (1958), Belgian fashion designer

"[Costumers] are extremely important in contemporary fashion… they dictate what they want and how they want it."
Bruno Basso (1978) and Christopher Brooke (1974), Brazilian-British design duo Basso & Brooke

"You have to create something that the customer feels an emotional attachment to when she looks at it and wears it… By being innovative you can keep customers."
Marios Schwab (1978), Austrian-Greek fashion designer

IT'S NOT WHAT YOU WEAR – IT'S HOW YOU TAKE IT OFF

rule
34

Never mind what you wear. After all, in the end, it is all about eventually becoming naked.

"Brevity is the soul of lingerie."
Dorothy Parker (1893-1967), American poet and writer

"All women's dresses, in every age and country, are merely variations on the eternal struggle between the admitted desire to dress and the unadmitted desire to undress."
Lin Yutang (1895-1976), Chinese writer

"A skirt is no obstacle to extemporaneous sex, but it is physically impossible to make love to a girl while she is wearing trousers."
Helen Lawrenson (1904-1982), American editor

"Is not the most erotic part of the body wherever the clothing affords a glimpse?"
Roland Barthes (1915-1980), French philosopher and literary critic

"My son has followed fashion since he was a punk. He and I agree that fashion is about sex. "
Vivienne Westwood (1941), British fashion designer

"There is no fashion for the old"

Classic line, which comes courtesy of French fashion designer Coco Chanel (1883-1971).

_____

"I grew up not wanting to grow up. Growing up seemed so terrible. [But] the most rewarding thing about being my age is that you don't have to take things quite so seriously."
Mary Quant (1934), British fashion designer

"I feel terrible for people over 35. They worry so about looking like mutton dressed as lamb. That's because they try to compete with their children, and that's a problem."
Barbara Hulanicki (1936), Polish-born fashion designer and founder of clothing store Biba

"I'm looking forward to growing old. Ponytails look good with white hair."
Karl Lagerfeld (1938), German fashion designer

"There's very little in the shops for people of my generation – every shop is trying to copy each other's idea of youth, and none of us stays young forever. I think it's depressing to see old people dressing in young people's clothes, but older people don't have any contemporary icons, that's the problem."
Celia Birtwell (1941), British textile designer

"A woman is as young as her knees."

Mary Quant (1934), British fashion designer

"I am getting older. The good thing, as far as my work is concerned, is that the older I get, the younger my brand gets. My customers are getting younger and younger as I get older and older. The only two disadvantages are that you have less time ahead of you and that physically you don't look that good. But everything else is better."
Diane von Fürstenberg (1946), Belgian-born fashion designer

"My biggest inspiration is old people. Their style is not pretentious. Their cord jacket might be a little worn, have elbow patches, but they're like 'I've been on the planet this long, this is my style'."
André 3000 (1975), American rapper, actor and designer behind label Benjamin Bixby

Blue and green should never be seen

Blue and green should never be seen without something in between. Navy and black do not match. And apparently combining brown with black is whack. As French style guru Madame Genevieve Antoine Dariaux points out, color combinations, or clashes, are subject to fashion: "A shade or combination which seems impossible to us today is quite likely to enchant us tomorrow."

———

"I can remember how daring it was considered when Dior first combined brown and black in the same ensemble, but now this harmony is considered a classic, as is navy blue with black."
Madame Genevieve Antoine Dariaux (1914), French style guru

"One of the first fashion stories I wrote, back in 1986, was about the strange union of black and navy, a rather bruised looking combination of tones. But the mix worked… But black and brown? I'd pass."
Cathy Horyn (1957), American fashion critic

"I love wearing navy and black together and have just done a print with blue and green in it. I don't play by the rules…"
Alice Temperley (1975), British fashion designer

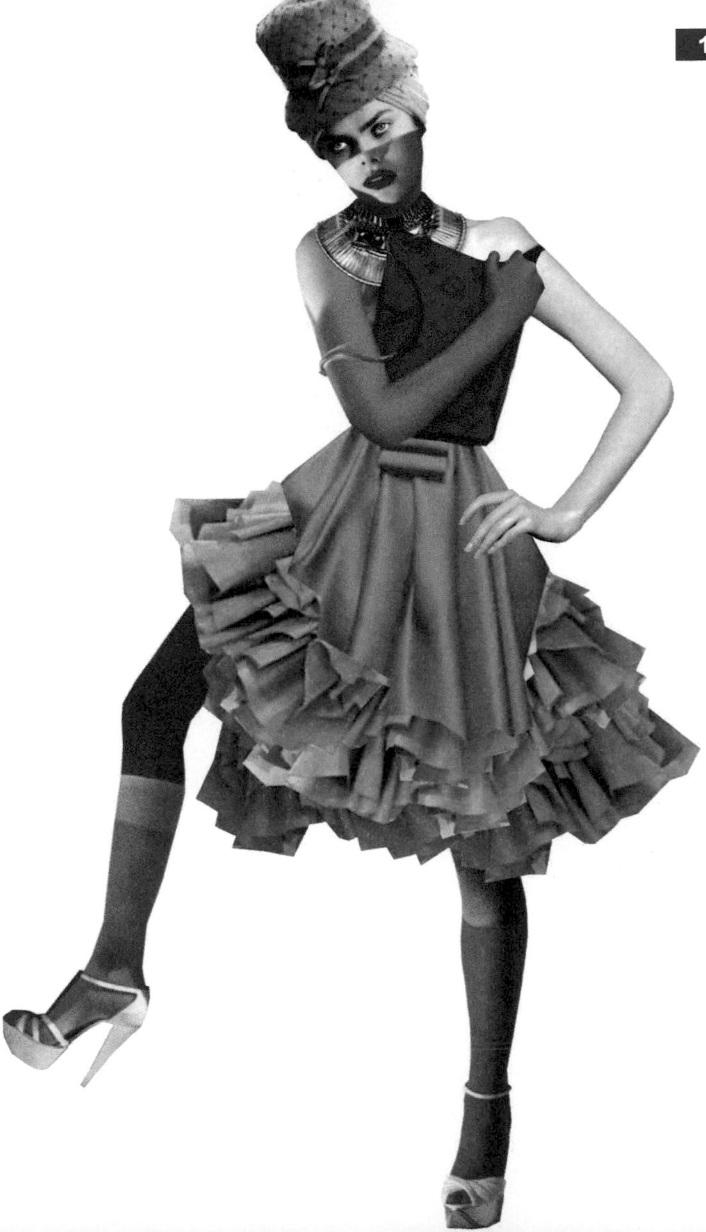

Satin and sequins are eveningwear

There was a time when glam was the domain of eveningwear. But not anymore. And according to British fashion editor Laura Craik we have Dries Van Noten, Christophe Decarnin at Balmain and Miss Carrie Bradshaw to thank for making "sequins acceptable options for day." Bless 'em.

"I've been called the Sultan of Sequins, the Rajah of Rhinestones and the King of Glitz. I probably have more titles than any other designer."
Bob Mackie (1940), American fashion designer

"Evening is a time of real experimentation. You never want to look the same way."
Donna Karan (1948), American fashion designer

"I want perfection, from the set to the shoot to the show, down to the sequins."
John Galliano (1960), Gibraltarian-British fashion designer

"Could anything be more modern than sequins for day?"
Scott Schuman a.k.a the Sartorialist (1968), American fashion blogger

"I don't understand why more people don't wear sequins – they're wonderful under a spotlight."
Brandon Flowers (1981), American frontman of The Killers

"Having rules of what's appropriate is dated. It's all about blurring the lines of day and evening wear, high end and low."
Alexander Wang (1984), American fashion designer

Function, not fashion

It's been called the fashion equivalent of the form follows function dictum. The idea is that a design's functional requirements should prevail over purely aesthetic concerns.

"Fashion is a function of lifestyle, and style a function of quality, integrity and timelessness."
Ralph Lauren (1939), American fashion designer

"It's about turning clothes designed for function into fashion."
Ralph Lauren (1939), American fashion designer

"Having a few pairs of boots, which can go with a variety of lengths, is really functional."
Valerie Steele (1955), American fashion historian

"Uniforms are fundamental to menswear. Fashion is all about the combination of function and putting on a show – and wearing clothes as a uniform."
Stefano Tonchi (1959), Italian-born style editor

"Follow function, not fashion. A good bag should have a clasp or a buckle only if it's got a purpose. The bells and whistles of women's bags just don't sit right in menswear."
Charlie Porter (1973), British fashion editor

"A hat is where function meets fashion."
Ann Watson, fashion director at NYC's Henri Bendel

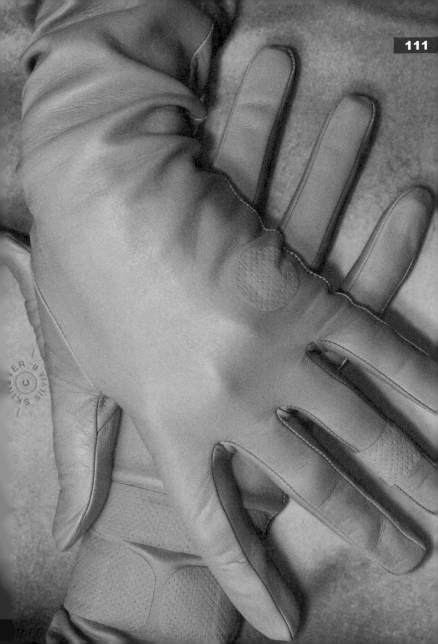

MATCH YOUR TIE WITH YOUR SHIRT

rule 39

Many men struggle with this one, but it is really quite simple. A striped shirt is best paired with a single-colored tie. If you insist on wearing a patterned tie on a patterned shirt, make sure the pattern on the tie is bolder than the one on your shirt. And as for clip-on and bow ties: they're just an unnecessary evil that should be avoided at all times.

"A well-tied tie is the first serious step in life."
Oscar Wilde (1854-1900), Irish poet, playwright and author

"I have a hankering to go back to the Orient and discard my necktie. Neckties strangle clear thinking."
Lin Yutang (1895-1976), Chinese writer

"Tie-wearers of all nations unite. Cast off the rope that binds you. Risk your neck. Liberate yourself and venture forth into open-collar paradise."
HRH Prince Claus of the Netherlands (1926-2002), removing and throwing away his tie at an award ceremony

"The expulsion of tieless diners from restaurants has more to do with their refusal to wear a social label than their attempt to expose their Adam's apples."
Desmond Morris (1928), British zoologist and anthropologist

"If men can run the world, why can't they stop wearing neckties? How intelligent is it to start the day by tying a little noose around your neck?"
Linda Ellerbee (1944), American journalist

"I do not mean to suggest for a moment that all it takes to be a top executive is a custom-tailored European suit. You also need the correct shirt and tie."
Dave Barry (1947), American author

DRESS FOR THE OCCASION

Dress for the occasion, as well as the destination.

—————

"The Queen's attitude is that she must always dress for the occasion, usually for a large mob of middle-class people. There's always something cold and rather cruel about chic clothes, which she wants to avoid."
Hardy Aimes (1909-2003), British fashion designer and dressmaker to Queen Elizabeth II

"**MY** NUMBER-ONE BELIEF WHEN DESIGNING UNIFORMS IS THAT IF YOU WANT TO LOOK LIKE A MANAGER, THEN DRESS LIKE A MANAGER. DRESS FOR THE OCCASION."

Peter Morrissey (1962),
Australian fashion designer

"I was brought up in Harrogate, so I'm used to walking in the country. I like to get dressed up in waterproof leggings, walking boots and plus fours for a country walk. I like to dress for the occasion, but whether I've actually got it right or not is another thing."
Oliver Spencer (1968), British fashion designer

"It's toppers and tails for Ascot. Boaters and bow ties for Henley. And anything goes for Wimbledon."
David Winder, Christian Science Monitor (1985)

To be / beautiful,

Tight corsets, chemical peels, butt implants, suffocating neckties, strict diets, uncomfortable heels, botox injections, breast augmentations. There seems no limit to the amount of suffering people are willing to endure in the pursuit of beauty.

"The French say that we must suffer if we would be beautiful, and this appears to have been and to be the opinion of most peoples, savage or civilized. Beginning with hair, we find that savage, like civilized, men and women will not let their hair follow its natural bent nor keep its natural color."
The New York Times, 1881

one must suffer

"I'm having surgery today to have my face cleaned up. But it will take some fancy stitching to make me all beautiful again!"
Patsy Cline (1932-1963), American country music singer

"I was bored with myself. I was bored with those oversized Japanese clothes where you can eat whatever you want. I mean, I'm in fashion, so I have to adapt myself."
Karl Lagerfeld (1938), German fashion designer on why he went on a diet

"I personally would not have plastic surgery. What the hell for? It looks ridiculous."
Calvin Klein (1942), American fashion designer

"I'm addicted to cosmetic surgery!"
Janice Dickinson (1955), American model and self-proclaimed first supermodel

Don't mix prints and patterns

The rule is never mix prints and patterns. But if you insist on bending or indeed breaking this classic fashion rule, at least make sure that the color schemes match.

"If you're going to mix prints and patterns, then anchor the look with to-die-for shoes"
Isaac Mizrahi (1961), American fashion designer

"Don't mix too many floral designs together – you will look like a garden."
Trinny Woodall (1964) & Susannah Constantine (1962), British fashion advisors and television presenters

"Print is an essential aspect of my work. The development of a new print for the season can kick-start an entire collection… I like to contrast and counterbalance color and print in unusual combinations combining the natural with the man-made – the contrast between design, fabric and decoration is the strongest inspiration of all."
Matthew Williamson (1971), British fashion designer

"Fashion is made to become unfashionable."

The transitory nature of fashion, summed up beautifully by French fashion designer Coco Chanel (1883-1971).

"So soon as a fashion is universal, it is out of date."
Marie Von Ebner-Eschenbach (1830-1916), Austrian author

"Fashion is a form of ugliness so intolerable that we have to alter it every six months."
Oscar Wilde (1854-1900), Irish poet, playwright and author

"Judging from the ugly and repugnant things that are sometimes in vogue, it would seem as though fashion were desirous of exhibiting its power by getting us to adopt the most atrocious things for its sake alone."
Georg Simmel (1858-1918), German sociologist

"Fashion fades, only style remains the same."
Coco Chanel (1883-1971), French fashion designer

"Art produces ugly things, which frequently become more beautiful with time. Fashion, on the other hand, produces beautiful things, which always become ugly with time."
Jean Cocteau (1889-1963), French poet, artist and filmmaker

"Fashions are born and they die too quickly for anyone to learn to love them."
Bettina Ballard (1903–1961), editor American Vogue

"Only the minute and the future are interesting in fashion – it exists to be destroyed."
Karl Lagerfeld (1938), German fashion designer

"Fashion will be in fashion for a long time."
Angelique Westerhof (1969), director of the Dutch Fashion Foundation

Shoes and belt must always match (and so should your socks)

This is basically the male equivalent of the rule 'Shoes and bags must always match.'

"Socks play an incredibly important role in a man's life."
Oscar Wilde (1854-1900), Irish poet, playwright and author

"I have always dressed according to certain Basic Guy Fashion Rules, including: 'Both of your socks should always be the same color.' Or they should at least both be fairly dark."
Dave Barry (1947), American author

"With a suit, always wear big British shoes, the ones with large welts. There's nothing worse than dainty little Italian jobs at the end of the leg line."
David Bowie (1947), British musician

If you've got it, flaunt it

rule
45

Nothing wrong with playing up your best assets. Although it's always nice to leave something to the imagination. After all, it's a fine line between sexy and slutty.

"As you grow older, cover up. Aging flesh is not appealing."
Edna Woolman Chase (1877-1957), American editor-in-chief Vogue

"The trouble with most Englishwomen is that they will dress as if they had been a mouse in a previous incarnation… they do not want to attract attention."
Edith Sitwell (1887-1964), British poet and critic

"It's always better to be looked over than over-looked."
Mae West (1893-1980), American actress

"Fashion is in a terrible state. An overdose of too much flesh."
Geoffrey Beene (1924-2004), American fashion designer

"A woman's dress should be like a barbed-wire fence: serving its purpose without obstructing the view."
Sophia Loren (1934), Italian actress

"Women are wearing tight and sexy clothes again. It is the body-conscious mentality, and women are revealing every bulge."
Manolo Blahnik (1942), Spanish-born British fashion and shoe designer

"It costs a lot of money to look this cheap."

Dolly Parton (1946),
American country singer and actress

"Today, fashion is really about sensuality – how a woman feels on the inside. In the '80s women used suits with exaggerated shoulders and waists to make a strong impression. Women are now more comfortable with themselves and their bodies – they no longer feel the need to hide behind their clothes."
Donna Karan (1948), American fashion designer

"If sluttiness is what you like, what's wrong with that? Why do we think being a slut's bad? Sluttiness is just a lot of freedom."
Tom Ford (1961), American fashion designer

"I suppose everything I do has sexual undertones, but I don't set out to make everything about sex. My clothes are more about sensuality. What I do is dress and beautify the body. My feeling is, if you have something beautiful, then show it."
Tom Ford (1961), American fashion designer

"As designers downsize menswear, the world gets an anatomy lesson."
Frank DeCaro (1962), American writer and performer

Horizontal stripes make you look fat

In 2008 a group of British scientists made a shocking discovery. Their study showed that contrary to popular belief horizontal stripes do not make you look fat. In fact, quite the opposite is true: horizontal stripes make you look thinner. That's another fashion myth dispelled.

"I can't wear stripes or bright colors because they make me expand."
Giorgio Armani (1934), Italian fashion designer

"[In the Middle Ages] stripes were the devil's clothing. The dress of prostitutes, of hangmen. They were considered transgressive… There is still a good stripe and a bad stripe today: when the banker's pinstripes become thick, like the bands you sometimes see on Al Capone, they're negative."
Michel Pastoureau (1947), French historian and author of the book The Devil's Cloth: A History of Stripes and Striped Fabric *(2001)*

"Stripes are an easy way to have some fun with your look. I always think of David Hockney – the way he dresses, with striped shirts and striped socks. It's a way to dress with flair but stay within the classic vernacular of men's wear."
John Bartlett (1963), American fashion designer

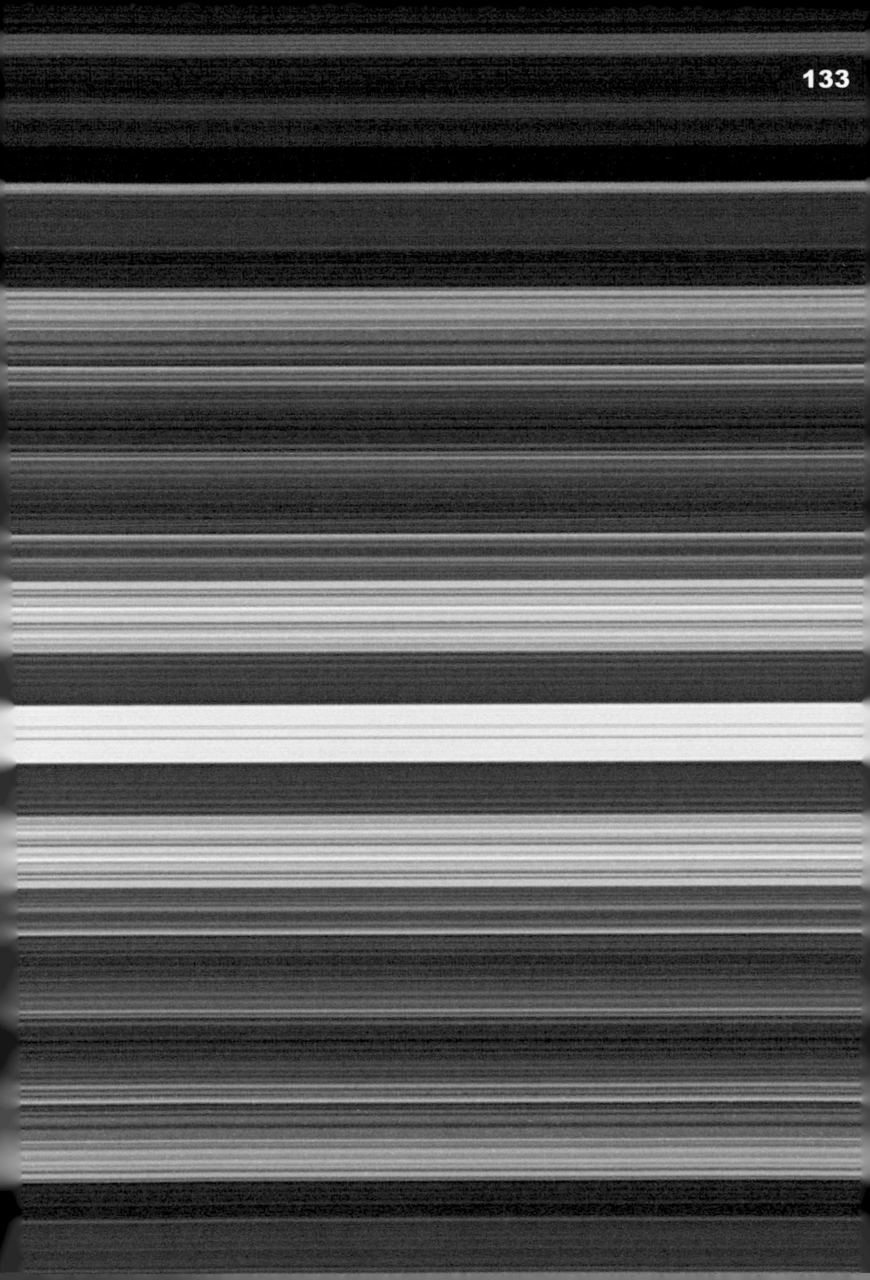

Wear the clothes, don't let them wear you

You know you're in trouble when the clothes on your back make more of an impression than you do. Nobody wants to look or indeed feel like a human clothing hanger, which is why clothes should never overpower the person wearing them.

"The dress must not hang on the body but follow its lines. It must accompany its wearer and when a woman smiles the dress must smile with her."
Madeleine Vionnet (1876-1975), French fashion designer

"There is much to support the view that it is clothes that wear us and not we them; we may make them take the mould of arm or breast, but they would mould our hearts, our brains, our tongues to their liking."
Virginia Woolf (1882-1941), British writer

"Look for the woman in the dress. If there is no woman, there is no dress."
Coco Chanel (1883-1971), French fashion designer

"Never fit a dress to the body but train the body to fit the dress."
Elsa Schiaparelli (1890-1973), Italian-born French fashion designer

"Our clothes are too much a part of us for most of us ever to be entirely indifferent to their condition: it is as though the fabric were indeed a natural extension of the body, or even of the soul."
Quentin Bell (1910-1996), British art historian and author

"The dress must follow the body of a woman, not the body following the shape of the dress."
Hubert de Givenchy (1927), French fashion designer

"The fashionable woman wears clothes. The clothes don't wear her."
Mary Quant (1934), British fashion designer

"Over the years I have learned that what is important in a dress is the woman who is wearing it."
Yves Saint Laurent (1936-2008), French fashion designer

"Many actors wear my clothes, because they don't like dated clothes. I think they like to be themselves in their everyday life, not to be wearing very flagrant designs. They like the absence of the design. You can't see it, so you forget about it. And the personality of the person wearing the clothes is more important."
agnès b. (1941), French fashion designer

"Women and men should always interpret clothes according to their style, be ironic and self-confident and let clothes take a supporting role to their personality. A dress should never look like it's overpowering the wearer."
Domenico Dolce (1958) and Stefano Gabbana (1962), Italian fashion designers

fashion is architecture: it is a matter of proportions

Leave it to Coco to come up with yet another fabulous fashion one-liner, this time on architectural fashion and engineered clothing.

———

"Dressmaking is the architecture of movement."
Pierre Balmain (1914-1982), French fashion designer

"The dress is a vase which the body follows. My clothes are like modules in which bodies move."
Pierre Cardin (1922), Italian-born French fashion designer

"Dressing a woman or man one must think in terms of lines, volumes, proportions. It is exactly the same as 'dressing' a space. The difference, the most important one, is that for the fashion designer the work of reference is the human body, an object in motion."
Gianfranco Ferré (1944-2007), Italian fashion designer, known as 'the architect of fashion'

"Hips are absolutely key to every shape I do, because whatever you do at the top or bottom, you want to keep it slim and narrow on the hips. One thing is for certain: No one, man or woman, wants big hips."
Tom Ford (1961), American fashion designer

"Modern fashion is less the proportions, more the elements which touch the person, their nervous receptors. That is why the latest trends are seen in accessories."
Igor Chapurin (1968) Russian fashion designer

"I am very fascinated by all the ways you can highlight, distort and transform the natural silhouette with clothes and accessories."
Sandra Backlund (1975), Swedish fashion designer

Don't wear too many colors at once

Unless you've been cast as the lead in the musical *Joseph and the Amazing Technicolor Dreamcoat* there is absolutely no reason to walk around looking like a human color wheel.

———

"The beggar wears all colors fearing none."
Charles Lamb (1775-1834), British essayist

"The best color in the whole world is the one that looks good, on you!"
Coco Chanel (1883-1971), French fashion designer

"I like light, color, luminosity. I like things full of color and vibrant."
Oscar de la Renta (1932), American fashion designer

"It's really easy to get colors right. It's really hard to get black – and neutrals – right. Black is certainly a color but it's also an illusion."
Donna Karan (1948), American fashion designer

"I love color, black does nothing for me."
Italo Rota (1953), Italian architect

"Color makes me happy. If I feel yuk, I wear black but I like the fact that color gets me noticed. If I walk past builders and don't get a bit of abuse, I am disappointed."
Henry Holland (1983), British fashion designer

Hemlines rise and fall with the stock market

Miniskirts mark a well-performing market. Low markets mean longer skirts. That is, according to the so-called hemline theory or index, which was coined back in the 1920s by American economist George Taylor.

"In difficult times fashion is always outrageous."
Elsa Schiaparelli (1890-1973), Italian-born French fashion designer

"Never in the history of fashion has so little material been raised so high to reveal so much that needs to be covered so badly."
Cecil Beaton (1904-1980), British fashion and portrait photographer

"Fashion anticipates, and elegance is a state of mind... a mirror of the time in which we live, a translation of the future, and should never be static."
Oleg Cassini (1913-2006), French-born American fashion designer

"The miniskirt enables young ladies to run faster, and because of it, they may have to."
John V Lindsay (1921-2000), American politician and former mayor of New York City

"Fashion is never in crisis because clothes are always necessary."
Achille Maramotti (1927- 2005), Italian fashion entrepreneur and founder of Max Mara

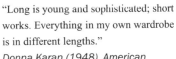

"Long is young and sophisticated; short works. Everything in my own wardrobe is in different lengths."
Donna Karan (1948), American fashion designer

"I like it when fashion – meaning self expression, creativity, spirit – is stronger than a crisis. It's not about ignoring the recession, but on the contrary, it's about reacting against it. It would be silly if I did not."
Christian Lacroix (1951), French fashion designer

"Every season I take the opportunity to convey a much larger message than just hemlines and trends."
Kenneth Cole (1954), American fashion designer

"Fashion is a part of the world and part of history. It's not a meaningless swirl of meaningless clothes. They reflect the times."
Valerie Steele (1955), American fashion historian

"Fashion is an expression and a reaction. It's a reflection, and even a proposal, on the current situation of our society."
Helmut Lang (1956), Austrian fashion designer

Break the Rules

rule
51

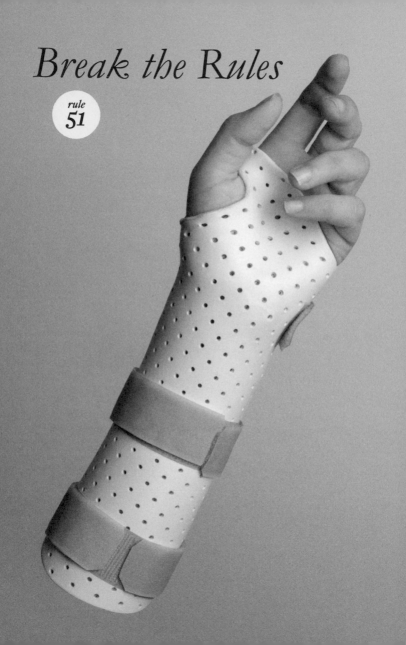

You need to know the rules before you can break them, which is why we close (and not open) with this one.

———————

"There are no rules for inspiration, you have to have a quality view on things and my curiosity helps me to find inspiration in the most unconnected of strange situations. But there is no rule, or only one: Keep your eyes open."
Karl Lagerfeld (1938), German fashion designer

"I have always believed that breaking rules is what makes clothes interesting. It is what I've done in different ways for my entire career. I love mixing fabrics and shapes in unexpected ways – the classic with the modern, the rugged with the elegant. There are no limits, as long as it's done with a certain taste level."
Ralph Lauren (1939), American fashion designer

"I think fashion is about suspense and surprise and fantasy. It's not about rules."
Wolfgang Joop (1944), German fashion designer

"I think that we need to laugh at everything once in a while. All these rules, all these things that we've been discussing about fashion – to me, when people talk about issues it's all a matter of pro-choice. You've got to be able to allow people to choose whatever they want."
Marc Jacobs (1963), American fashion designer

"I hate rules and formulas. That's so boring. It's the opposite of creativity. Rules are ridiculous things that are meant to be broken."
Philip Treacy (1967), British hat designer

"The fashion world is an industry, and we had to learn to stick to certain codes and rules."
Viktor Horsting (1969), Dutch fashion designer and one half of Viktor & Rolf

CONTRIBUTORS

1 Rianne Duursma
- Linda van de Wiel
- FOTOPEER
(www.fotopeer.nl)
- Kelly Henkelman

2 Christian Tagliavini
(www.christiantagliavini.com)

3 ontwerpplus (cc)
(www.ontwerpplus.nl)

4 Carlos Buendia
(www.carlosbuendia.com)

5 timparkinson (cc)
(www.flickr.com/photos/timparkinson)

6 Tara K. Dougans
(www.taradougans.com)

7 Hartog & Henneman
(www.hartoghenneman.com)

8 Silvia B.
(www.skinover.biz / www.silvia-b.com)

9 Hanneke van Leeuwen
(www.hannekevanleeuwen.com)

10 Jasmin Fuhr
(www.jasminfuhr.de)

11 Victoria Ball
(www.victoria-ball.co.uk)

12 Saba Gedda
(www.beckmans.se/saba-gedda)

13 Haabet

14 Bela Borsodi
(www.belaborsodi.com)

15 Atypyk
(www.atypyk.com)

16 Hanne van der Woude
(www.hannevanderwoude.nl)

17 Lina Bodén
(www.linaboden.se)

18 SERIAL CUT™
(www.serialcut.com)

19 Victor Pyk
(www.pyk.eu)

20 Pink Sherbet Photography ⓒⓒ
(www.flickr.com/photos/pinksherbet)

21 Rachel Oxley
(www.racheloxley.com)

22 Lizzy Peters
(www.lizzypeters.nl)

23 Lisa Karlsson

24 Carine Brancowitz
(www.carinebrancowitz.com)

25 Sarah Illenberger
(www.sarahillenberger.com)

26 Montana Forbes
(www.montanaforbes.com)

27 Mario Sughi
(www.nerosunero.org)

INDEX BY SUBJECT

INDEX BY NAME

Thanks to:
Premsela, Dutch Platform for Design and Fashion (www.premsela.org)
Lemon Scented Tea (www.lemonscentedtea.com)
AMFI Amsterdam Fashion Institute / Mint Magazine (mint.amfi.nl)
Unit (www.unit.nl)